The School Hits of the 70s

Wise Publications
part of The Music Sales Group
London / New York / Paris / Sydney / Copenhagen / Berlin / Madrid / Tokyo

Published by
Wise Publications
14-15 Berners Street, London, W1T 3LJ, UK.

Exclusive distributors:
Music Sales Limited
Distribution Centre, Newmarket Road,
Bury St Edmunds, Suffolk, IP33 3YB, UK.

Music Sales Pty Limited
120 Rothschild Avenue, Rosebery,
NSW 2018, Australia.

Order No. AM988262
ISBN 13: 978-1-84609-825-3
ISBN 10: 1-84609-825-4
This book © Copyright 2007 Wise Publications,
a division of Music Sales Limited.

Compiled by Nick Crispin.
Edited by Fiona Bolton.
New arrangments by Joel Payne.
Music processed by Paul Ewers Music Design.

Cover design by the Design Corporation.

Printed in the EU.

Your Guarantee of Quality:
As publishers, we strive to produce every book
to the highest commercial standards.

Particular care has been given to specifying
acid-free, neutral-sized paper made from pulps
which have not been elemental chlorine bleached.

This pulp is from farmed sustainable forests
and was produced with special regard for the environment.

Throughout, the printing and binding have
been planned to ensure a sturdy, attractive
publication which should give years of enjoyment.

If your copy fails to meet our high standards,
please inform us and we will gladly replace it.

www.musicsales.com

Blame It On The Boogie

Words & Music by Elmar Krohn, Thomas Meyer, Hans Kampschroer,
Michael Jackson Clark & David Jackson Rich

1. My
3. This

(1.) ba - by's al - ways danc - ing,___ and it would - n't be___ a bad___ thing, but
(2.) na - sty boo - gie bugs___ me, but some - how it___ has drugged me,
(3.) ma - gic mu - sic grooves me, that dir - ty rhy - thm fools___ me, the

Boogie Wonderland

Words & Music by Jon Lind & Allee Willis

You say your prayers though you don't care. You dance and shake the hurt.

I find romance when I start to dance in boogie wonderland. I find romance when I start to dance in boogie wonderland.

I find___ ro - mance___ when I___ start to dance_

_ in boo - gie won - der - land.___

Dance! Ooh, ooh, ooh, ooh, dance! Boo - gie won - der -

- land,___ ha, ha!

Repeat and fade

Daddy Cool

Words & Music by Farian & Reyam

♩ = 120

N.C.

She's cra-zy like a fool.____

What a-bout it, Dad-dy cool?____

Fm   E♭

Fm   E♭

Fm   E♭   Cm

Spoken: She's cra - zy 'bout her Dad - dy.

Oh, she be-lieves in him.

She loves her Dad - dy.

D.S. al Coda

Coda

Dad - dy, dad - dy cool.____

Dancing Queen

Words & Music by Benny Andersson, Stig Anderson & Björn Ulvaeus

2. A - ny - bo - dy could be that guy,_____
3. You're a tea - ser, you turn 'em on,_____

night is young and the mu - sic's high,
leave 'em burn - ing and then you're gone,

with a bit___ of rock mu - sic
look - ing out___ for an - oth - er,

ev - 'ry - thing___ is fine.
a - ny - one___ will do.

You're in the

mood for a dance,___

and when you get the___ chance,_____

22

23

Disco Inferno

Words & Music by Leroy Green & Ron Kersey

Burn,___ ba - by, burn! Burn,___

ba - by, burn! Burn,___ ba - by, burn!

Burn,___ ba - by, burn!

1. To my sur - prise,___ lis - ten, one hun-dred stor - ies___ high.__

2. 3. Sa - - tis-fac - tion came__ in a chain__ re - ac -

- tion. Peo - ple___ get-ting loose,___ y'all, they're get - ting

I could-n't get e - nough till I had__

26

ba - by, burn! Burn the moth - er down! Burn,___ ba - by, burn!

Dis - co___ in - fer - no! Burn, ba - by, burn! Burn the moth - er down.

moth - er down. Up a - bove my head, I hear

mu - sic in the air. That makes me

I Will Survive

Words & Music by Dino Fekaris & Freddie Perren

strong   and I learned how to get a - long.___ And so you're

1. back   from out - er space_____   I just walked
3. me   some - bo - dy new._____   I'm not that

in to find___ you here___ with that___ sad look up - on___ your face. I should have changed
chained up lit tle per - son still in love___ with you.___ And so you

___ that stu - pid lock,___ I should have made___ you leave your key___ if I'd -'ve known___
felt like drop-pin' in___ and just ex - pect me to be free.___ Well, now I'm

31

I'm In The Mood For Dancing

Words & Music by Mike Myers, Ben Findon & John Puzey

Rockin' All Over The World

Words & Music by John Fogerty

(1.) here we are and here we are and here we go, all a-board and we're
(2.) gid-dy up and gid-dy up and get a-way, we're go-ing cra-zy and we're
(3.) gon-na tell your ma-ma what you're gon-na do, come on out with your

hit - ting the road,__ here we go,_____ rock-ing all__ o - ver the world.__
go - ing to day,__ here we go,_____ rock-ing all__ o - ver the world.__
danc - ing__ shoes, here we go,_____ rock-ing all__ o - ver the world.__

2. A -   And I like_

___ it, I like__ it, I like__ it, I like__ it, I la - la - like__ it, la - la - like,_ here we go,_

To Coda

rock-ing all__ o - ver the world.__

42

Intstrumental

D.S. al Coda

3. I'm

la - like,___ here we go,_____ rock-ing all___ o - ver the world.___

And   I   like___

Repeat and fade

In The Summertime

Words & Music by Ray Dorset

mind.

Have a drink, have a drive,

go out an' see what you can find.

Play 4 times

2. If her
3. We're not
4. When the

Verse 2

If her daddy's rich take her out for a meal;
If her daddy's poor just do as you feel.
Speed along the lane, do a ton, or a ton an' twenty-five.
When the sun goes down you can make it, make it good in a lay-by.

Verse 3

We're not grey people, we're not dirty, we're not mean,
We love everybody but we do as we please.
When the weather's fine we go fishing, or go swimming in the sea.
We're always happy, life's for living, yeah! That's our philosophy.

Verse 4

When the winter's here, yeah! It's party time;
Bring a bottle, wear your bright clothes, it'll soon be summertime.
And we'll sing again, we'll go driving or maybe we'll settle down.
If she's rich, if she's nice, bring your friends an' we'll all go into town.

Kung Fu Fighting

Words & Music by Carl Douglas

50

kung fu___ fight - ing, huh! Those kids were fast as light - ning.___ In fact it was a lit - tle bit___ fright - 'ning, yeah, yeah, but they fought with ex - pert___ tim - ing.___

1.

2. There was

52

Verse 2:
There was funky Billy Ching
And little Sammy Chong
He said here comes the big boss
Let's get it on
He took a bow and made a stand
Started swaying with the hand
A sudden motion made me skip
Now we're into a brand new trip.

Everybody was kung fu fighting *etc.*

Lay Your Love On Me

Words & Music by Mike Chapman & Nicky Chinn

My Sharona

Words & Music by Douglas Fieger & Berton Averre

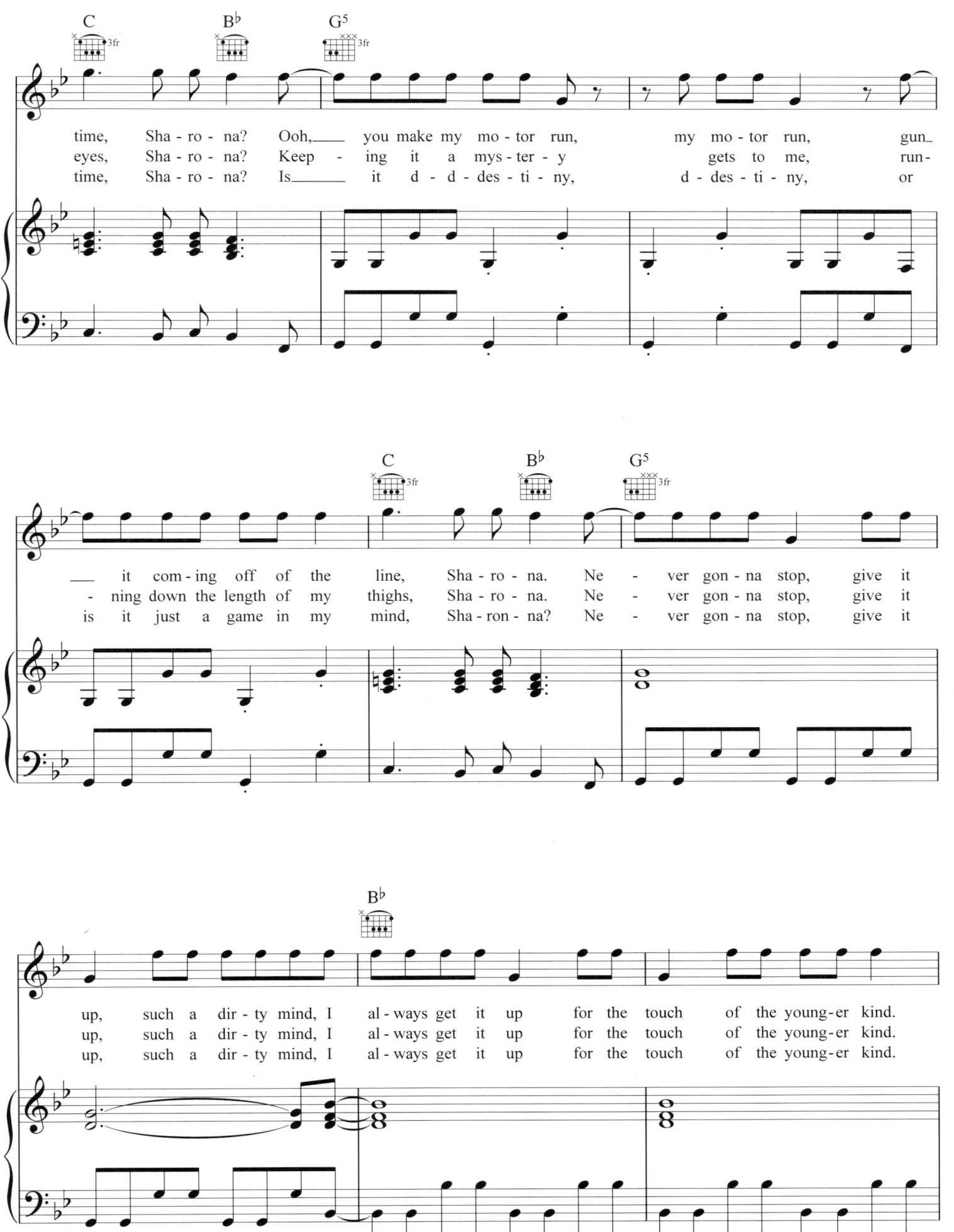

D.S. al Coda

Coda

M-m-m-m-m-m-m-m-my, my,___ my-

-y   -y, wow!   M-m-m-my Sha-ro-na.

61

School's Out

Words & Music by Alice Cooper, Michael Bruce,
Dennis Dunaway, Neal Smith & Glen Buxton

Well we got___ no choice,___ all the girls___
Well we got___ no class,___ and we got___

and boys,   making all   the noise,
no prin - ci - ples.   And we got   no in - no - cence.

To Coda

'cause they found   new   toys.   Well we
we can't e - ven think of a word that rhymes.

C   E♭

can't sa - lute ya, can't find a flag.   If that don't suit ya, that's a drag.

Gm   B♭   F/G   Gm

School's   out   for   sum - mer.

School's out for - ev - er.

School's been blown to piec - es.

No more pen - cils, no more books.

That's The Way (I Like It)

Words & Music by Harry Casey & Richard Finch

Cm

That's the way ah ha ah ha I like it,— ah ha ah ha,

that's the way ah ha ah ha I like it,— ah ha ah ha.

That's the way ah ha ah ha I like it,— ah ha ah ha,

1, 2, 4.

that's the way ah ha ah ha I like it,— ah ha ah ha.

Verse 2:
When I get to be in your arms
When we're all, all alone.
When you whisper sweet in my ear
When you turn, turn me on.

Verse 3: ad lib.
Babe, oh babe
That's the way, ah ha, that's the way, ah ha
Babe, oh babe
That's the way, ah ha, that's the way, ah ha.

Venus

Words & Music by Robert van Leeuwen

(1.) god-dess on a moun-tain___ top   was burn-ing like a sil-ver___ flame.
(2.) wea-pon were her crys-tal___ eyes,   mak-ing ev-'ry man_____ mad.

The sum-mit of beau - ty and love,   and
Black as a dark___ night___ she___ was,   got what no -

Ve - nus was her name.   She's got it.
- one else___ had.

Yeah, ba - by, she's got it.   Well,

2. Her

Ah.

Ah.

D.S. al Coda

76

You're So Vain

Words & Music by Carly Simon